Teaching Guide
the Faith

A CATECHIST'S GUIDE TO
CLASSROOM MANAGEMENT

Kim Duty

PAULIST PRESS
New York / Mahwah, NJ

Cover & book design by Lynn Else

Library of Congress Cataloging-in-Publication Data

Duty, Kim.
    Teaching the faith : a catechist's guide to classroom management / Kim Duty.
       p. cm.
    ISBN 978-0–8091–4400–6 (alk. paper)
    1. Classroom management. 2. Christian education of children. 3. Catechists. I. Title.
    LB3013.D88 2007
    371.102′4—dc22

2007003051

Published by Paulist Press
997 Macarthur Boulevard
Mahwah, New Jersey 07430

www.paulistpress.com

Printed and bound in the
United States of America

Contents

From Me to You
v

1. What Will the Children Be Like?
1

2. How Do Children Learn?
11

3. How Should I Organize My Teaching Space?
19

4. How Do I Manage My Class and Plan My Lessons?
30

5. What Kids Wish You Knew
46

And Finally...
55

From Me to You

Dear New Catechist,

As I begin this book, I am thinking about you, the reader. And I'm wondering if you have the same thoughts and feelings as almost every new catechist does…

What *ever* made you say yes to your director of religious education (DRE), faith-formation director, pastor, or whoever it was that asked you if you would be willing to teach in the religious education program this year? How are you going to do it? You're already busy, you're not a teacher, and right now you're frantically trying to think of ways to get out of it. You don't know enough about the Catholic faith yourself, let alone trying to tell others about it. You're not a "churchy" person: you don't read the Bible; maybe you don't even pray every day. People who know you are rolling their eyes at the thought that you are going to teach religion. You're the last person that should be doing this. Why on earth did you ever say yes? And what on earth were you thinking when you said yes?

If the paragraph above sounds like you could have written it yourself, then count yourself among the thousands of people each year who approach the religious ed classroom with fear and trepidation, unsure of themselves, their abilities, and their faith.

Throughout my years of recruiting and training catechists, no one has ever come up to me and said, "I'd like to be a catechist this year. I'm up-to-date on classroom techniques; I have a strong background in scripture; I'm knowledgeable about Catholic doctrine; I'm a person of great faith; and I'm eager to share this with a class of students." It just doesn't happen. What *does* happen is that someone just like you somehow finds him- or herself roped into a program and ends up not only liking it, but volunteering to come back the following year. Yes, it really happens, time after time, year after year. And yes, even though it seems far-fetched, you may find it happening to you too.

It might help to know that you have a lot in common with some very famous people who also might have wanted to say no, but ended up saying yes anyway: people like Moses, who absolutely, positively, did not want to return to Egypt; Jeremiah who pleaded with God that he was too young to be a prophet, and discovered that it really didn't matter when God had a plan for him; and then there was Mary, who in spite of the cost trusted in God and said yes. Nothing has ever been the same since. Nor will it be for you.

Where do you begin? Right here, right now, with this book. In it, you'll find some very basic, practical techniques, tips, and ideas on a variety of topics that will get you off to a good start. You'll learn some things about child development and how children learn; about the catechetical process and lesson plans; about your classroom set-up and what to do when you get there. Reading this book won't make you an educator or a theologian. But it is my hope that you will find in these few pages what you need to help you feel confident as you face your first year of teaching.

You may not realize this yet, but it is God who has called you to teach this year. You may never know the reason why God needs you to reach this child, to touch this heart, to challenge this mind, to plant this seed, but you are where God wants you to be. And he will be with you just as he was with Moses, Jeremiah, and Mary. You can count on it.

Kim Duty

1
What Will the Children Be Like?

Being a teacher begins and ends with the children who are in your class. Who are they? What are they like? What can you expect of them? And what do they have a right to expect of you?

Most of the volunteers in religious education programs are parents. You're probably one of them and more than likely you already have a good understanding of children. However, you may be asked to teach children who are older than your own. Or, the years have flown by so quickly that it is hard to remember exactly what your own children were like when they were younger. The following paragraphs will give you a glimpse of what the children in your class might be like. While growth and development differ with each individual child, and not all classes of children will be the same, here are some things that you can expect of most children in a specific age-group.

PRESCHOOLERS

Preschool children are warm and friendly, and like to please their parents and teachers. They are active and want to *do* things. You'll want to keep this age-group involved by using play dough, building with blocks, singing songs accompanied with simple movements, playing ball and active games, finger painting—anything that uses as many of their senses as possible. They like to imitate adults and enjoy playing with toy tools or kitchen utensils. They like to play dress-up. Preschoolers enjoy the activity itself and most of the time are not as interested in the final results as we are. This is something to bear in mind when working with small children. A finger painting of your church building may look like random colors, but to them, it is just perfect. They will be eager for you to admire it.

Preschoolers learn best from concrete experiences rather than from verbal explanations. They want to see and touch rather than hear about. This is not the group that will sit for long periods of time while you do the talking. They have short attention spans and, in most cases, an activity should last no longer than five to eight minutes.

You will find a wide range of abilities among the children in this age-range class. Some children will seem very capable while some may still have a lot of toddler characteristics. A child who is almost five years old will be quite different in abilities from the child who has just turned four. Be aware of these differences as you plan your lessons. For the first week or two, use very simple activities. Each child will then have a positive experience and you will be able to observe the children to learn what kinds of activities they can do.

KINDERGARTNERS

Kindergartners have many of the same characteristics of preschoolers. They are eager learners and they usually "love" their teacher. They will want to talk to you, to sit near you, and to be with you. Friends and family are very important to the five-year-old, and most of the time, they relate well with each other. Kindergartners love visiting all kinds of places: friends' homes, zoos, fire stations, stores, and so on. This is an ideal time to take the children on their first short tour of your church or rectory. Don't forget to take them on a tour of the building in which you are teaching. They will enjoy seeing all of the other rooms.

As with preschoolers, you will find that five-year-olds are quite different in their abilities. Some will be able to read and write a little, while others may not know how to do either. Some may be able to print letters or to cut and paste with only a little guidance, while others will need a lot of help. Keeping these facts in mind when you are planning and teaching your class will make it a better experience for all of the children—and for you too.

Kindergartners respond well to a set routine and are very comfortable when each class follows the same schedule—a plus for you as you plan. They like stories but take them very literally, so choose carefully when using any Scripture stories. Five-year-olds work well in organized group activities, and can spend ten minutes, and sometimes even longer, when engrossed in a project.

FIRST-GRADERS

Six-year-olds are enthusiastic learners. They are experienced in a classroom situation and know what to expect when they get there. They can follow simple directions and are able to complete some tasks independently. They are usually willing and eager to participate in new activities, but they are becoming more sensitive to criticism. They are beginning to notice when they can't do something as well as another child. At this age, their teacher is very important and they will want to please you.

Six-year-olds' fine and gross motor-skills are developing rapidly. You'll find most of them are able to print, color, cut, and paste fairly well. They are learning to read, and some children may even be able to read simple books. You'll be amazed at the difference in the children from your first day of class to the last.

First-graders are beginning to develop their own preferred learning styles, which means that you will want to use a greater variety of activities in class. There will be lots more on learning styles in a later chapter!

SECOND-GRADERS

Second-graders will look to you for approval and acceptance. Seven-year-olds are beginning to form groups of friends and they are concerned about fitting in with the group. This is the age where you may find cliques, where some kids are "in" and some kids are "out." You'll need to pay close attention to this, especially if you have children from different schools in your religion classes. Your help in getting them to know each other and to bond as children who are part of the same parish will make all of the children feel that they belong. This need continues throughout the grades.

Second-graders have a strong sense of fairness. They see things as black or white. If there is a rule set down, they want everyone to follow it and follow it exactly. This is an age where children "tell" on each other. In spite of this, seven-year-olds continue to be very sensitive to criticism, so use caution when correcting a child's work or actions.

Most second-graders are reading independently. They are able to do more complex projects than first-graders and they follow directions well. While abilities continue to vary, most children can print their names and complete written activities. They are becoming more expressive and they are eager to tell you every detail of what they've seen or done. At times, you may find yourself having to cut short their sharing in order to move on with the rest of the lesson!

THIRD-GRADERS

You'll find that third-graders are outgoing and friendly. Their self-esteem continues to develop, but they still feel a strong need to be accepted by the group. Be on the lookout for children who seem alone or isolated. You'll need to make a special effort to be sure that they are an integral part of any group activities.

Third-graders continue to improve their communication and educational skills. They are usually good listeners, and they are learning to read facial expressions and body language. They watch to see your reactions to their words and actions.

Eight-year-olds work well in groups, and they enjoy participating in group activities. They like challenges. They love games like "Who Am I?" and puzzles with clues to help them find the answers. They are able to work well independently and enjoy completing projects on their own.

Third-graders are beginning to see things from another's point of view. They are also able to understand cause and effect—that actions have consequences. You will see your third-graders' sense of morality grow this year.

FOURTH-GRADERS

Fourth-graders are an interested and interesting group of young people. They are very individual in their thoughts and ideas. You'll find that they enjoy discussing and exploring issues. They are becoming more intellectually curious. As with all children, they find their friends increasingly important. They are becoming more critical of themselves and compare themselves with those around them. This is a time to emphasize cooperative rather than competitive activities in class. Help each child to recognize that he or she each has something to contribute to the group.

In school curricula, the level of sophistication in fourth grade educational materials is significantly different from those used in third grade. Nine-year-olds can usually read and write well. They can perform fairly complex tasks. This is a great time to involve the class in more long-term projects, rather than activities that can be completed within a class period.

Fourth-graders have an increased sense of right and wrong. They are aware of the motivation and intentionality of their own actions and those of others. Build on this awareness in teaching them to be kind to each other. You will have many interesting discussions with your fourth-graders, especially in the area of morality.

FIFTH-GRADERS

Fifth-graders are usually energetic and enthusiastic. For the most part, they cooperate well, both with you and with their classmates. They still are sensitive about what others think of them, their ideas, and their actions, so continue to affirm them whenever possible.

Ten-year-olds respect their parents and their teachers. They feel strong bonds with their families and with their friends. Humor and laughter are often a part of their interaction with each other, which makes them a lot of fun to have in class.

There is often an increasingly wide range of intellectual ability among fifth-graders, and the children themselves are becoming more aware of this. Feelings of inadequacy can be significant in children when they compare themselves with others. Be sure that your lessons give everyone a chance to succeed.

Fifth-graders' interests are becoming more diverse and individual. Some may play on the soccer field, others on a chess board, and still others on video games. Make it a point to find out what your fifth-graders like to do, and use this information as you help students to relate church teachings to their lives.

SIXTH-GRADERS

Sixth-graders are experiencing growth spurts that will continue for the next several years. They're changing mentally, physically, emotionally, spiritually, and morally. These changes have an impact on how they act from day to day. One day they are up and the next day they are down.

The peer group is all important. Eleven-year-olds want to fit in with their friends and pay more attention to fads in how they dress or speak. They look for role models and have a strong interest in sports figures, movie stars, and other popular figures. This is a great time to teach about historical and contemporary saints and heroes, especially those who have met great challenges and succeeded.

Eleven-year-olds are growing in their ability to think abstractly. Most eleven-year-olds will not accept all information as absolute or right, just because you or the Church says it is. They question and want to think things out on their own. Give them the freedom to discuss their thoughts and opinions as you express the mind of the

Church on a topic. They are beginning to think about and make decisions on their own. Be sure to present them with a firm foundation of faith that they can use in making their decisions.

SEVENTH- AND EIGHTH-GRADERS

Exuberance, enthusiasm, awkwardness, and insecurity are all words that describe the junior high student. It is often a time of confusion as bodies and minds are growing and changing. Feelings of uncertainty and inadequacy abound as some children find themselves maturing at a faster or slower pace than their classmates. This is the time to use your X-ray vision to see the feelings of self-consciousness and lack of self-esteem in your students. Be very conscious of how fragile many junior high kids are and how much they need to know that God loves them for who they are.

Seventh- and eighth-graders are an exciting and ener-gizing group to teach. They are developing critical think-ing skills, which help them as they question and challenge our Christian beliefs, and as they try to make them their own. Ask thought-provoking questions. Encourage dis-cussion and debate. Help them to discover that this has been the pattern for all people of faith. A study of church history shows time and time again how challenging and diverse ideas have come together and strengthened our Church.

CONCLUSION

I hope that taking a look at some of the characteristics of the different age-groups has given you some idea of what you might expect to find in your own class. But please remember, these are by no means absolute. In your class, you may find your students act more like children who are in a lower or upper grade. All classes and all children are different. One year your third-graders might like paper-and-pencil activities and working in their textbook. The next year's third-graders groan when you pass out papers or books. They'd rather role-play and do projects. However, in spite of some specific differences, you will find that they still have many things in common with all other eight-year-olds.

Knowing a little more about what to expect of the children in the various grade levels should give you a better idea of what grade level you'd like to teach. Some people love to sing and play with the younger children. Others want to work with children who are able to read and write. Still others enjoy the interaction found in working with older students. Where do you feel you would be most comfortable? Being able to relate well with the age-group you're teaching makes for a much better experience both for you and for the kids!

2
How Do Children Learn?

The previous chapter dealt with child development and briefly illustrated what we can expect of children at various ages. In this chapter we focus on the educational dimension: how do children learn?

It is absolutely amazing how much has been discovered during the past twenty years about how children learn. The insights of scientists, educators, physicians, and psychologists have had a tremendous impact on the way children are educated, the way textbooks are written, the way teachers are trained, and the way classrooms are organized. These new understandings have changed the way we teach children in religious education as well.

The textbooks used in religious education today are very different from those used a generation ago. Today's texts are written by teams of experts who understand not just theology and pedagogy, but also the Church and the child. Publishers use the best educational research available to create programs that make teaching and learning a successful experience at every grade level. Catechists and the children they teach have benefited enormously. Even brand-new catechists can be confident that what they teach is educationally and doctrinally sound. In other words, relax. You don't need to be a theologian or a professional educator to be a catechist. Just be yourself.

LEARNING STYLES

Learning styles are simply different ways of learning. Most people have a preferred learning style, a way in which they best receive and process information. For example, people approach the task of assembling things in different ways. Some prefer to thoroughly read the written instructions before they begin. Others like to have someone read the instructions to them as they work. Still others put aside the written instructions and jump right into the task.

There are three types of learning styles: the visual learner, the audio learner, and the kinesthetic learner.

The Visual Learner

The visual learner learns best by seeing. These children prefer to sit at the front of the class and use the textbook. They seem absorbed when they are reading handouts or watching videos. They like written instructions. Just pass out the paper and they'll begin reading right away, even before the rest of the papers have been given out. They don't wait for you to read the directions to them. Visual learners make lists of things, and in the upper grades, they'll be the ones taking notes in class. Visual learners have an easy time remembering things that they've *seen*.

The Auditory Learner

The auditory learner learns best by hearing. These are the children who listen to what you say. They learn more when they can hear the text read aloud, rather than by reading it silently. They enjoy discussions and debates. Auditory learners are most attentive when you are teaching by talking or lecturing. They prefer oral instructions, and when presented with an activity, they will often wait until you tell them what to do.

Auditory learners are usually quite sociable. They verbalize their thoughts and feelings well. They look interested when listening, and you'll notice this especially when you're reading a story. Your auditory learners will become absorbed in it. Auditory learners have an easy time remembering things that they have *heard*.

The Kinesthetic Learner

The kinesthetic or tactile learner learns best by doing. They learn through moving and touching. They are active children and find it hard to sit still for long periods of time. Kinesthetic learners' attention wanders when they are just listening or reading. They want to be *doing*. They need to be involved in an activity, making something, role-playing, writing on the board, working with manipulatives, using puppets, and singing action-oriented songs. Kinesthetic learners will learn history better by making a time line, than by just reading about it or listening to someone tell them about it. Kinesthetic learners have an easy time remembering things that they have *done*.

Don't make the mistake of thinking that working with kinesthetic learners means just arts and crafts or projects. Reaching kinesthetic learners means developing ways to keep them actively involved in the learning experience.

HOW TO TEACH USING THE THREE STYLES

How do the three styles work in your classroom? Let's look at an example. You're next chapter is on the Ten Commandments. A visual learner might learn them best from reading them over and over in the textbook. An auditory learner might learn them more easily by hearing them read aloud and repeated. The kinesthetic learner might learn them more easily by arranging them in order.

Each one of these techniques, while primarily geared to a specific learning style, helps all of the children in your class. We learn in many different ways, not just in our preferred way. When you use all three, your teaching will be well-rounded and give everyone in your class the best possible opportunity to learn and understand the material.

You'll find that some lessons naturally lend themselves to just one particular learning style. For instance, a tour of the church is more kinesthetic, a guest speaker is more auditory, and a chart of the liturgical year is more visual. All children will utilize all three learning styles to some extent, so there is a certain amount of overlapping. Don't think of learning styles as completely separate from each other. Rather, think of them as flowing back and forth as they work together to maximize each child's learning experience.

All major publishers of teachers' manuals consider learning styles when they are developing and writing lesson plans. And now you will probably find yourself thinking about the various learning styles of the children you teach as you plan your weekly lessons and choose from among the options presented in your manual.

MULTIPLE INTELLIGENCES

In 1983 Dr. Howard Gardner, an educator from Harvard University, presented a theory of multiple intelligences that has had a huge impact on education. Dr. Gardner proposed that the way in which we measured intelligence was both limited and limiting. He felt that there are a variety of "intelligences" evident in people, not just the verbal and the logical, which are the two categories traditionally used in measuring intelligence. We all have different aptitudes, and there are many aspects to our intelligence. We are "smart" in various ways, not just those customarily used to decide our IQ.

At the present time, multiple intelligences include nine categories. It is useful to think of these categories as natural abilities or instincts rather than styles of learning. These are things that people just do naturally.

- *Verbal.* A child with verbal intelligence is good at reading, writing, and thinking in words. They like to write, to tell stories, to memorize, to talk, to read, to discuss, to debate, and so on. Maya Angelou is a good example of a person with verbal intelligence.
- *Logical.* A child with logical intelligence reasons things out. They like to solve problems and to work with numbers and experiments. They like material to be taught in sequence, or to have the opportunity to find an answer on their own. Albert Einstein is a good example of someone with logical intelligence.
- *Visual.* A child with visual intelligence thinks in images and pictures. They like to look at pictures, to draw and design, and to imagine. Pablo Picasso is a good example of someone with visual intelligence.
- *Kinesthetic.* A child with kinesthetic intelligence is good at anything that involves movement: dancing, athletics, and eye-hand coordination. They like to move around and to use their hands to create or build. Magic Johnson is a good example of someone with kinesthetic intelligence.
- *Musical.* A child with musical intelligence is very sensitive to sounds, accents, and rhythm. They like music and often play an instrument or sing. Mozart is an example of someone with musical intelligence.

- *Interpersonal.* A child with interpersonal intelligence is good at understanding and relating to people. They like to interact with others. They have lots of friends and are very sensitive to others' feelings and ideas. Mother Teresa is a good example of a person with interpersonal intelligence.
- *Intrapersonal.* A child with intrapersonal intelligence is very self-aware and self-confident. They like to work alone and sometimes shy away from others. Thomas Merton is a good example of a person with intrapersonal intelligence.
- *Naturalistic.* A child with naturalistic intelligence recognizes and appreciates the natural environment. They like to be involved with nature, with plants and animals. Charles Darwin is a good example of a person with naturalistic intelligence.
- *Existential.* A child with existential intelligence wonders about things. They like to ponder deep questions. Aristotle is a good example of a person with existential intelligence.

All the research on how children learn and understand reinforces what we, as Christians, have known all along: We are wonderfully and marvelously made. We are created with different skills and talents. We are created with different abilities and ideas. No one gift is better than any other, and each of us is created the way that God wanted us to be.

In your class you will find all kinds of children with all kinds of abilities and talents. Some will be easy to reach, and others may challenge your skills and ingenuity. Some will hang on to your every word, and others will question everything you say. Some days will be good, and others will leave you doubting your abilities. Some days you will be great, and some days you will be boring. But through it all, God will be right there, at your side. Look over at him every once in a while. He'll be holding up a cue card, ready to help you out!

3

How Should I Organize My Teaching Space?

In real estate, the key to success is location, location, location. In classroom management, the key to success is planning, planning, planning. It makes all the difference in having a successful year.

So far in this book, we've taken a look at the children you'll teach and the way that they learn. Now it's time to take that information into the place where it all comes together—your classroom.

THE CLASSROOM

Once you've found out what grade level you'll be teaching, the next practical question you should ask is "Where will I be teaching?" Are you sharing a classroom that is used during the day by Catholic school students? Are you using a parish meeting room? Some other parish space? If your exact room has not yet been assigned, your director of religious education should be able to give you some basic information about what kind of a room it

19

will be. Visit the possible locations. Go into the rooms and look around. Picture yourself teaching your class in the room.

If you will be teaching in a Catholic school classroom, these are some questions you should consider:

- Is the grade level taught in the room the same level that you will be teaching? If not, is the furniture suitable for your grade level?
- Are there desks? How many? Will there be enough desks for your class? How are they arranged? In rows? In groups? Are the students' names fixed on the desks? Anything else?
- Is there a space in the room for children to gather together? Is the room crowded? Is there anything in the room that seems like it may be problematic?
- Is there any audiovisual equipment in the room? An overhead projector? A video or DVD player and screen? CD player? Anything else?
- How many bulletin boards are there? Is there one in the front of the room? If so, is there a ledge in front of the bulletin board where you can prop up a poster or foam-core board?
- Is there a prayer table? If so, what is on it? If not, is there a small table in the room that could be used?
- Are there chalkboards or dry-erase boards in the room? Are markers or chalk available?

- What about supplies? Are there student Bibles that you might be able to share? Maps? Other religious education materials? Are there scissors? A pencil sharpener? Anything else?
- What about the teacher's desk? Is there a table in the front of the room that you might be able to use while you are teaching?
- Where are the restrooms in relation to the classroom? Where are the exits? Which exit is closest to the room?
- Are there any other special things that you might need or want in the room?

THE CLASSROOM TEACHER

If the classroom teacher was not present or available during your room visit, make arrangements to meet as soon as possible. Your DRE or the school principal may want to participate in any meetings with the teacher. If the room will be used by another religious education class on another day, it would be a good idea to include that catechist in the meeting as well.

When you meet with the teacher, bear in mind that the primary use of the room is as his or her classroom. Be sensitive to the fact that while the school is a parish facility, the regular teacher is there all day, every day, while you will be there for only an hour or so each week. Making a teacher aware that you recognize this fact often goes a long way in establishing a good working relationship. Here are some questions that you might consider discussing at your meeting:

- Have there been any problems in the past when religious education classes used the room? If so, what were they? How were they handled?
- Is there anything in the room (students' projects, things written on the board, etc.) that should not be touched or moved? How will the teacher let you know about these things during the year?
- What classroom supplies and books are available that can be shared with your students? Bibles? Storybooks? Prayer or songbooks? Anything else? Where are these materials kept? How many are there?
- What is available for you to use? What about the A/V equipment? Where is it kept? How does it work? Where are the plugs and extension cords? Are there videos, DVDs, and CDs that you may use?
- What about the prayer table? Will you be able to use it as is, or should you bring your own supplies? Is it all right to light a candle in the room?
- Where are the chalk and markers stored? Is there a small cubby where you might store your materials such as extra pencils, scissors, paper, and so on, rather than having to carry them with you?
- When and how will you communicate during the year?

If you are fortunate enough to be teaching the same grade level, ask about how you might help each other during the year. You may find a video that works well with a unit theme, while the teacher may have an idea for a story that fits perfectly. One of you may know a guest speaker who can speak to both groups on the same day. The teacher may be using something special for class that he or she could keep for you to use, or vice versa. Maybe you could even have your classes work together on a service project. There are lots of possibilities that will help each of you.

The important thing is to establish a working relationship with the classroom teacher. Sharing each other's expectations and concerns at the beginning of the year, and setting up a means of communication during the year, will help make the year easier and better for both of you.

A ROOM IN THE PARISH HALL

What if you're teaching in a parish facility rather than the school? Ideally, these rooms are designed as multipurpose rooms, which make them more flexible to use than a regular classroom. Here are some things you should look for as you tour the room:

- What kind of furniture is there? Tables? Chairs? Desks? Are they movable? Are they an appropriate size for your class? Is the space large enough? Who is responsible for setting up the room?

- Are there chalkboards or dry-erase boards in the room? Are markers and chalk readily available? Where are they stored?
- Are there bulletin boards in the room? If so, will any or all of them be available for your use?
- Are there bookshelves? Bibles, songbooks, or other religious education materials available? If so, are there sufficient numbers for your class?
- Is there any audiovisual equipment in the room? If not, is any available? Where is it stored? Must it be reserved ahead of time? If so, how is that done? Where are the plugs and extension cords? Is there a screen?
- Is there a prayer table in the room? Will that be available for your use? If not, is there a table that can be used for that purpose? Is it all right to light a candle in the room?
- Where are the restrooms? The exits? Which exit is closest to the room?
- Is there a desk in the front of the room or a table that you can use for your materials as you teach?
- Is there a secure place where you can leave your materials and supplies from week to week?
- Who will be using the room immediately prior to and following your class?
- Will any other religious education classes be using the room? If so, what grade level will be using it?

If you will be sharing the room with another catechist who is teaching on your grade level, you may want to work together on bulletin boards, room setup, and so on.

PHYSICAL ENVIRONMENT

No matter where you are teaching, there are a few things that are essential to creating a good learning environment for your students. The chairs and desks must be suitable for your children. It is very uncomfortable to sit in a desk that is too small or too large. If you find yourself assigned to a classroom where this is the case, try to have your room changed. If that cannot be done, arrange to use chairs for your class. This may mean moving all of the desks to the back of the room. Lap desks or even pieces of foam-core board can be used for written activities, although they are much more difficult to use than tables. If that is all you have, you will need to curtail many written activities.

Be sure that there is adequate lighting in the room. The ability to darken the room is a plus when you are showing a video.

Be sure that all of the children can see you and the board without difficulty.

Be sure that your room has adequate ventilation. If your room has been used all day, try to open the windows to let fresh air into the room. Otherwise, your class may have some sleepy or lethargic children in it.

ARRANGING THE ROOM

Of course, the ideal is to have a room that is flexible and that can be arranged easily to meet your needs. However, if you are in a classroom with desks, there is still a lot that can be changed to make the room work for you.

Here are room arrangements that you might consider. They assume a class of fifteen students in a classroom with either twenty-five desks or four tables.

- *Traditional arrangement.* Five rows, five desks per row, three children per row: in this traditional arrangement, it is difficult to see all of the children and for the children to see you and the board. An easy solution is to have every other child move their desk a few feet to the right or left. This is easy do and easy to undo each week.
- *Semi-circles.* Rearrange the desks into five semi-circles of three, or three semi-circles of five, each with the open side toward you and the board. Position the back semi-circles to the left or right of the front ones. This arrangement takes time to set up, but is ideal for small-group discussions and projects.
- *U-shaped.* Arranging all the seats in the room into a single U allows the children to see each other and you, but it may require a lot of time to set up before class and undo after class.
- *Small circles.* Move the desks into sets of two, three, or four. (Absences will often provide differently sized

groups.) This is ideal for working in pairs or small groups.

- *Filled-up rectangular or round tables.* In this arrangement, the children are seated entirely around each table, meaning that some children will not be able to see you or the board without completely turning around. One solution is for you to walk around and between all the tables when you are explaining or discussing something. In this way, having to turn fully around isn't imposed on the same group of children every time.

- *Half-filled rectangular or round tables.* Here the children are seated on *just one side of the table,* facing front. This is a better arrangement than the above. The children still have a place to work, but they can see you and the board.

Use your creativity and imagination to develop an arrangement that works for you. One school teacher arranged the desks to form the number *50* during the week the school was celebrating its fiftieth anniversary. But remember, a lot of setup time means a lot of take-down time!

PRAYER TABLE

You'll want to have a prayer table in your room. This will be your gathering place for prayer at the beginning or the end of class. The table should be large enough to hold a candle, a bookstand, a bible, and a place for a symbol such as a palm branch, a photo, a basket of bread, a pitcher with water, and so on. You may want to add a vase of flowers, a pumpkin, or some other seasonal decoration. The table should be covered with a cloth. Some teachers have colored cloths matching the seasons of the church year. Others use a white cloth and change only the color of the candle; or perhaps they may add ribbons in the color of the seasons. A prayer table should be simple and free of clutter. It should be changed throughout the year to reflect what is happening in your class.

Think about where you might like to place your prayer table. A prayer table in the front of the room can visually assist with the lesson. A prayer table in the back of the room will provide a special place for prayer. Ideally, the prayer table is in a place where the children can easily stand and move around it.

YOUR CLASS KIT

Save yourself time, energy, and frustration by putting together a class kit at the beginning of the year and keeping it supplied all year long. You'll gather supplies for each individual project or weekly lesson as you need them, but this kit is your yearlong, "just in case" kit. There will always be a child in your class who doesn't have a pencil, a pen, a crayon, the textbook, and maybe even a tissue. With a class kit, you will be prepared to supply these last-minute needs!

Some teachers use a plastic box, others a tote bag. Whatever you use, it should be small enough for you to carry along with your other lesson materials, yet large enough to hold everything you'll need. Here are some items that you might find useful to include in your kit:

- Three or four sharpened pencils (those small miniature-golf pencils will do in a pinch) or pens
- A small box of crayons, magic markers, or colored pencils
- A pair of scissors
- A roll of tape
- An extra textbook
- Extra name tags
- Paper clips
- A notepad
- Tissues
- Small packets of premoistened towelettes
- Emergency activity sheets to use when you've finished everything you planned to do and there are still five minutes left until the end of class
- Anything else that you think you might need

An entire lesson plan can be interrupted, momentum lost, and time wasted while you search for an extra pen, pencil, or book for the child who has forgotten his or hers. Don't let this happen to you. Have an extra on hand. Don't forget to have the item returned to you at the end of class, so you'll have it ready and available for the next time.

4

How Do I Manage My Class and Plan My Lessons?

Years ago, when I first began my teaching career, my teaching supervisor told me, "Teaching isn't hard. If you can follow a recipe, you can teach. Just walk into the classroom, turn on the light, face the class, and smile!" There's a lot more to it than that, but what she really meant was, "Don't worry. It's not that hard. Just relax." Good advice.

GETTING TO KNOW THE CURRICULUM

The most important thing is to know what you will be teaching. As soon as possible, get a copy of the student text and the teacher's manual for your grade level. Put the teacher's manual aside for now and get to know the student book. This is the heart of what you'll be teaching this year.

Leaf through the book. Look at the table of contents and the pictures. Then, sit and read it. Try to find a time when you can read it all in one sitting. That will give you the total picture of the content and help you to see how each chapter and unit connect with and build on the others. It will also give you a feel for how the material is oriented to the age group you'll be teaching. In some cases, you may find the language simpler than you expected. In others, it may seem more sophisticated. In either case, you'll gain insights into what is age appropriate for your class.

It is very important to read through the entire book *before* you teach, rather than reading it chapter by chapter *as* you teach. You will already be familiar with much of what you are reading. However, you may also discover some areas of church history or doctrine that are presented differently from what you remember being taught, or perhaps even some that are new to you. Knowing that gives you a chance to do some reading and updating in advance of teaching, rather than at the last minute. Your teacher's manual will usually give you good background information for what is taught in each chapter, as well as providing references for further study. Being comfortable with the content will make you more comfortable in the classroom.

Another reason why it is important to know what you'll be teaching all year is that you'll have it in the back of your mind as you read, shop, and watch TV. You may see a TV show where a moral dilemma is presented, and realize that perhaps this is something that you can use with your sixth-graders when you are teaching morality. You may read about an injustice, a new saint being canonized, a natural disaster, or an enduring friendship. You may see a project that would be ideal for Advent, or hear about a speaker who might be able to visit your class. Being tuned into your lessons will help you to keep your eyes and ears open to a great variety of materials and ideas.

Expandable file folders are a great way to maintain and organize your finds. Have a section for each unit, or perhaps one for topics, such as prayer, morality, service projects, and more. Each time you see something that might work, clip it out or jot it down, and then file it away. You will find this "idea bank" an invaluable resource as you plan you lessons throughout the year. You may even find other teachers coming to you for ideas!

One you feel familiar with the content of the student book, take another look to see what additional features it has:

- Are there written activities included in the book?
- Does it have chapter or unit reviews?
- Are the vocabulary words in bold print on the page?
- Does it include prayer services?
- Does it have Bible stories or other kinds of stories?
- Are there information pages for parents?
- Is there a section on church feasts and seasons?
- How long is each chapter?
- Are there other features that stand out?
- Is there anything else about the book that you want to note?

The time you spend getting to know your student book is time well spent. There is no better way to get a handle on what you will be teaching and learning this year.

THE TEACHER'S MANUAL

This book is going to be your most valuable resource, so get to know it well. It has everything that you will need to know in order to teach successfully this year. Teacher's manuals are full of ideas and resources as well as lesson plans. These books have been written by all kinds of people who are experts in their fields. All that experience and knowledge are right there, when and where you need it. All you have to do is turn the page.

Most teacher's manuals begin with a special section written especially for you. These pages include many topics, both about catechesis in general and about your specific grade level. Don't skip over these. Read them carefully. They are invaluable and usually contain background on the philosophy of the program. You will find information about recent church teachings, as well as church documents that relate to catechesis, such as the *Catechism of the Catholic Church* and the *National Directory for Catechesis.* You will become familiar with the material you are teaching, and the material of the program as a whole. There will also be advice on interacting with parents, families, and students. Special features of your catechetical program will be explained, including ways to plan for the year, keys to the lessons, and the overall process that you will use to teach. Spend some time with these pages, since they illustrate the common format you will use to teach every lesson in the program.

Every program has a unique way of presenting the in-class catechetical process, but as with all teaching, there are certain elements that are essential to all of them. Most lessons involve three to five basic steps. First, there is an introduction ("This is what we're going to do today"), as well as a sharing of experiences. This is followed by the presentation of the material or content. Finally, there is a conclusion, which involves an integration of faith and life, a review of what was learned, any necessary clarifications, and a closing prayer.

The introduction helps you to set the framework for the lesson. It begins to focus attention on what you will be teaching and often gives you insights into what your children already know about it. This first step may be called "Exploring Life" or "Getting Ready," or something like that. In this step, you will tap into the child's experiences as they relate to the subject. This might be done with a story or questions, a written activity or a shared experience. For instance, if the lesson is on helping others, the manual may suggest that you begin with a story of people working at a food bank or at a clothing drive. The story or activity that you will be using is usually right in the student book. The story or activities will usually be followed by questions and discussion.

In the second step of the lesson you will be presenting the content to be learned. This step might be called "Learning Our Faith" or "The Church Teaches," or something similar. The information to be learned in the second step will always be found in the student book. Your manual will give you clear instructions on what to say as you present each part of this material to your students. This part of the lesson is where new vocabulary words will be introduced and where matters of doctrine will be highlighted. Often there will be a scripture story or reference.

The third step of the lesson focuses on integration and prayer. The content of the lesson will be meaningless to the students unless it is made relevant to their lives. Learning about the Good Samaritan won't make any difference unless we realize that the story is really showing us how we should love our own neighbors. This integration helps the children to make sense of what has been presented that day and gives them ways to make it a part of their lives. We don't just teach faith so that people can parrot back information. We teach faith to challenge people to change their lives.

Following the integration activities, the class closes with prayer. In most instances, the prayer service is included in the student book.

As you look over the teaching process in these teacher's pages, notice the supplementary information on each lesson page. This is usually found in boxes on the side or bottom of the page. The boxes may include additional background information, optional activities, resources, and other helpful information.

The teaching process is usually explained very well at the beginning of a typical teacher's manual. The steps of each lesson and the variety of additional helps are outlined with a care and expertise that greatly benefit teachers. The front of the manual is also the place where you will find some marvelous resources that have been created to enrich the subject matter of each grade level. These may include such things as classroom activity books, music, videos, posters, and a variety of other ancillary products that save you time when you are looking for a song or an activity that fits perfectly with the chapter. Check with your DRE to see which resources are available for you to use. This section of the manual was written to be a comprehensive and yet concise resource for catechists. If you're new to teaching, or new to teaching in this particular program, you're missing out by not using it.

THE FIRST DAY

OK, you've read the book, followed the directions in the teacher's manual, toured your classroom, and set up your emergency kit. Classes start today!

Get there at least fifteen minutes before the children arrive. Remember, you set the tone for the classroom. Arriving early gives you time to get everything ready. You'll be able to spend time greeting the students and showing them where to sit. You'll create a welcoming, relaxed atmosphere. What's more, the students will sense that you are organized and all set to teach.

Contrast this with the teacher who rushes in at the last minute and is still setting up the class while the students are arriving. The atmosphere is one of confusion and chaos. That is a recipe for disaster and one that can easily be avoided.

Sometimes it's hard to get there early, especially if you're driving your own children to the program. I know one smart and helpful DRE who reserved a room for catechists' children. They went in there, had a snack, and played a game while their parents were free to prepare for class. If your school does not have this kind of useful setup, suggest it to the DRE. Seventh- and eighth-graders are often eager to help, and this is a great way for them to be involved in your parish program.

Welcoming the Children

Decide ahead of time whether you will assign seats to the children or whether they can sit where they want. If they will have assigned seats, put each one's name tag at their place. As the children enter, explain that they can find their place by looking for their nametag. If seats are not assigned, then you may give the name tag to the children as they enter the room, and then invite them to sit where they wish.

You will find some "getting acquainted" activities in your teacher's manual. Be sure to spend some time at the beginning of class getting to know your students. Even though you may be eager to begin the lesson, this is an important part of your session. While you're getting acquainted with your students, notice what the children are like. Which children are talkative and which are quiet?

Which children seem alone and which are part of a group? Jot down your observations as soon as you can.

Setting the Ground Rules

Before you begin your first day, you should have a clear idea of what will and won't be acceptable in your classroom. You have only a short time together, and that time needs to be used for teaching, not correcting. Having a set of guidelines that everyone knows and understands will help you avoid problems before they start.

Some new teachers are hesitant about making rules because they don't want to be thought of as overly strict or unfair. Others are fearful that the kids won't like them. These may seem like good reasons, but having rules doesn't make you strict or unfair or unpleasant. Just the opposite. The more the children understand what is expected of them, the less time you will need to spend correcting them, and the more time you'll be able to spend affirming them.

The first day is the time to tell the students what the rules will be for the year. If you don't do it the first day, you'll spend the rest of the year trying to play catch-up. You'll need to set up two kinds of rules: one for "housekeeping" and the other for behavior.

Housekeeping rules are those that deal with leaving the room neat and orderly when class is over, bringing in the materials needed for that week, and so on. They may also involve where the children may wait before class, attendance, and other issues that pertain to the entire program.

Behavior rules deal with your students' interaction with each other and with you. These are crucial to creating an atmosphere of respect and cooperation in your room. Without them, little teaching, and little learning, can happen.

Don't be afraid to set standards of behavior that are important to you. When setting the rules, remember to make them specific and limited in number.

Typical classroom rules might be—

- Come to class with your book, your folder, and a pen or pencil every week.
- Raise your hand and wait until you are called on before speaking.
- Pay attention when others are speaking or reading aloud.
- Stop talking when I give a certain signal (for example, ringing the bell, flashing the overhead light). (This is a useful rule to have when the children are doing group work, or working on a project.)
- Treat others as you want to be treated.

Explain the rules on the first day of class. Post them where the children can see them, and put them up every week. If a child forgets to follow one of the class rules, you can gently remind him or her by referring to the chart. The idea is to let everyone know what is expected of them. You don't want to be authoritarian, but you need order so that you can teach. There is a huge difference between being controlling and having control.

Often teachers will involve their students in setting up the classroom rules. This works well, especially in the middle and upper grades.

SETTING TEACHING GOALS

Working without a goal is like setting out on a trip without knowing where you are going. How will you know when you get there? There is something satisfying about knowing what you want to accomplish, working step by step toward that goal, and then achieving it.

Setting goals for yourself as a teacher and for your students is a necessary step in the learning process. As a catechist, you have long-term and short-term goals. The long-term goal is one that all Christians share—to know, love, and serve the Lord. The short-term goal is what you want to accomplish with your students this year.

Some goals may be dictated by the grade level you are teaching; for example, your goal in second grade may be to prepare the children to receive Eucharist or reconciliation for the first time. Other goals may be parishwide, such as faith-sharing on the weekly Gospel. Be sure to talk with your DRE about what will be expected from you and from your students during the year. Is it important that the children complete the textbook? If so, then you will need to work out a plan to accomplish that within the year. Is the goal to involve the children in some kind of outreach or service project? If so, then you will need to incorporate that into your plan for the year.

You may also have your own specific goal for your class. Perhaps your children don't know traditional prayers. You may want to spend a part of each class reviewing and learning them. Or, you may find that your children don't know how to use the Bible. If so, you may want to spend a few minutes each week practicing with the children. Your goal may be to give each child the chance to participate in class each and every week, or to help the students start and continue a journal—whatever it is, plan how you will incorporate it into your class each week. Think long-term. The year goes by very quickly.

LESSON PLANS

Lesson plans are *the* essential element to successful teaching. Thankfully, in today's teaching manuals, almost all of the work has been done for you. Use the lesson plans in the manuals. They were created by experts, and they work!

The lesson plans in your manual follow the catechetical process (using three, four, or five steps) as outlined above. All of the lesson plans will be set up exactly the same way.

The opening page or two of the lesson will include background information on what will be taught. This may include church doctrine or tradition, historical information, or other essential facts. Review all of the material found there. If you feel that you need to know more about the subject, use the suggested resources or ask your DRE for help. You cannot teach what you don't know.

Afterward is usually an overview or outline of how the lesson will be taught. It includes objectives for each part of the lesson, a summary of what you will do in each part of the lesson, and the materials that you will need. There will be additional helpful information regarding the vocabulary words, time limits for each section, and recommendations for coordinating components such as videos, music, black-line masters, and more.

Next is the lesson itself. Detailed instructions for *everything* you need to say and do are printed right alongside the reprinted page from the student's book. Read through the lesson carefully. Think about the students in your class as you plan. Is there someone who has an experience that relates to the lesson? Does the lesson seem to have enough variety to appeal to your students? This will become easier as the year progresses and you get to know your students better.

Note the additional ideas and activities that are suggested. Highlight any that you will use. Gather the materials that you will need to teach the class.

The best time to begin planning your next class is shortly after you've taught the preceding lesson. You will then have time to think about it during the week and be on the lookout for things that you can use in class. Make it a habit to plan your lesson early, and you'll need only a short period of time to review your lesson plan just before you teach. You never know what will happen at the last minute.

COMMUNICATION WITH PARENTS

Our task as catechists is to support what is happening in the home. We respect the parents as the primary educators of their children. We support them by teaching specific content in an organized and systematic way. Both catechists and parents have a role to play in the education of children. Faith formation doesn't happen in a classroom, but rather in the lived experience of everyday life. The ideal is when parents and catechists work together to complement and support what is being taught by the other.

Most parish programs have a plan in place to communicate with parents about the program and what is happening in it. It is always a good idea for you to keep in touch with parents as well. You might like to consider the following suggestions:

- Write a welcoming letter introducing yourself to the parents. Give an overview of what you will be teaching during the year. Let them know if you want the children to have any additional supplies, such as a folder, or crayons. Tell them how they can get in touch with you. Let them know what your expectations are for their child. Ask if there is anything special that you should know about their child to help you make his or her classroom experience more rewarding.

- Use e-mail. Ask the parents for their e-mail address so that you can send them periodic updates on what is happening in class.
- Enlist their help in projects you have planned, such as field trips, art activities, and so on.
- Invite parents to come and read a story to the class.
- Invite them to participate in a scheduled prayer service.
- Ask them how *they* would like to be involved in classroom projects or events.
- Ask them to be on the look-out for things that you can use in class.
- Ask them for their suggestions.

EVALUATION

Your parish DRE may have a plan in place for a yearly evaluation of the religious education program. In addition to that, it's a good idea to create your own private, ongoing evaluation of how you're doing.

At the end of every class take a few minutes to think about how the lesson went. Was there anything that was especially successful? Was there anything that didn't work? Did the activities take a shorter or longer time than expected to complete? What would you do again next year and what would you eliminate from that lesson? What, if anything, would you add or change? Write it down in your manual while it is fresh in your mind. Make notes to yourself so that you will have them to use next year. (Yes, I know, you only said that you would teach for one year, but do this, just in case...)

Check your students' progress on a regular basis as well. Begin each week by calling to mind what was taught the previous week. At the end of each chapter or unit, don't limit your reviews to what was just taught. Integrate questions from prior chapters and units. Have the children think up questions to ask each other. These ongoing reviews need not be intimidating to the students. They can and should be simple and fun.

Once you've taught your first few classes, you'll have a good feel for what works and what doesn't. You'll have settled into a routine with the class. Lesson planning will be easier and you'll realize that you are on the road to a successful year.

Your classroom is where everything you have prepared takes place. You are the teacher. You set the tone. You set the standards. You create the atmosphere. You plan the lessons. You choose the activities. You make it all happen.

Be yourself. You know your strengths and limitations. Use them to your advantage. Don't waste time comparing yourself with other teachers. Let your own light shine, and the light of the Lord will shine through you.

5

What Kids Wish You Knew

Everything included in this book so far has been written from an adult's perspective. You've read what I, an experienced catechist, think will help you as a new catechist. But what about the kids you'll be teaching? If they had a chance, what would they like to say to you? After all, they are the reason why we have become catechists in the first place.

Being a catechist is very different from being any other kind of teacher, coach, or Scout leader. Everything we do in religious education is based on a profound respect for each person as an individual, created by God and loved by God. That changes everything from the way we treat children, to the way we deal with parents, to the way we treat each other. We are aware that the child we teach is unique and fragile, precious and vulnerable, made in the image and likeness of God. As catechists we take responsibility to lead that child to a better understanding of God. This is an awesome responsibility, and we can only accomplish it with God's help and constant support.

We look at the children in our classes through the eyes of faith. In one of her songs, Christian pop star Amy Grant speaks of wanting people to say that "she has her father's eyes." She sings of wanting to be the kind of person who sees things through God's eyes, not her own. We try to do the same thing.

We show the children what a difference faith does make by the kind of lives we live. People expect more from us in a religious education program, not as teachers, but as Christians. We are modeling for the children, and for each other, how an adult Christian acts—and that is never easy. In the days of the early Christians, people were invited to learn about their faith not through books, or questions and answers. Rather, they were invited to "come and see." That's what we do in religious education programs. We invite children into an environment that is based on Jesus. They learn as much from being with us as they do from what we say. This is not something to be taken lightly.

When the children "come and see" in your classroom, what are they hoping for? Deep down, past their request for a party every week and no homework, what kinds of things would they like you to know and remember about them?

Perhaps the first thing the children are looking for is an opportunity to be successful. They want to have a chance to succeed and to be accepted for who they are. They want you to like them, to respect them, and to judge them by who they are now, this year, not by who they were last year, or by what last year's teacher said about them.

We don't want to be judged by who we were, but by who we are. The same is true of the children. Remember that kids are in process, in formation (aren't we all?), and yet sometimes we let former actions stand in the way of helping the child to grow and develop today. There is a Peanuts cartoon that illustrates this well. Lucy is once again holding the football for Charlie Brown. Every other time Lucy has held the ball for Charlie, she has moved it just when he is about to kick. This time, Charlie misses it again, but this time Lucy hadn't moved it. When questioned, Charlie Brown says, "I guess the past got in my eyes." Don't see what *was,* see what *is.*

Actors sometimes find it difficult to move on to play a new role when they have long been identified in another. Richard Thomas will always be "John-Boy" to some people and Carroll O'Connor will always be remembered as "Archie Bunker." It is hard to shed that identity.

We don't mean to do it, but sometimes we do that same thing with children. We think of them as they *were,* not as they *are.* Children are changing and growing. They need to have a chance to be seen as the person they are becoming, rather than the person they have been.

Your expectations of success have a lot to do with whether you have a successful class or not. One year a teacher received her class list. Next to each name was a number ranging from 130–150. She looked at the numbers in surprise. Never before had she had a class with such high IQs. She immediately set to work. She planned lessons that were more challenging, more interesting, and more creative than any she had done before. Her classroom became an exciting place to be. The children were learning better than any other class she had taught. It was by far the best year she had ever had in teaching. Imagine her surprise when, at the end of the year, she discovered that those numbers next to the children's names were not their IQs, but their locker numbers!

Children perceive what we think of them without our ever saying a word. When we create a positive atmosphere of affirmation and acceptance, we send them a powerful message. Children do try to meet our expectations. Expect the best from your class and give every child a fresh start every year. If they could put their wishes into words, here's what they might say:

"If you didn't like my brother or sister or you don't like my mom, don't take it out on me. Or if my brother or sister was smarter than I am, or a better reader, or didn't do their homework, don't act as though I'm exactly like them. I'm not!

"Treat us all fairly, but not exactly the same. Don't shortchange me, and sometimes give me a break. If I can't read well out loud, then don't ask me to do it. Ask me to do something that I can do. Think about what you say to me, and how you look at me. Sometimes the way you treat me is the way the other kids do. I want you to treat me better, as Jesus would. I know that you know things about me that I wish you didn't…but let me know that it doesn't matter."

When we teach in our parish programs, we sometimes find ourselves with children we'd rather not have in our classes. Maybe they've had a fight with one of our own children, or maybe they've hurt them in some way. Perhaps you've had a disagreement with one of the parents, and some discomfort still lingers. If this happens to you, then get over it. Trust that God has put this child in your care for some reason, perhaps even to teach about reconciliation and humility. Then take a deep breath and decide that you are going to move beyond what was, to what can be. We expect Jesus to be more than fair with us. How can we be less with the children?

Being fair to the children sometimes means looking beneath the surface to what lies underneath. Not all children are cute and sweet and adorable. They come in all sizes, shapes, and dispositions. We can't judge just by what we see. As the saying goes, "It's what's inside that counts." Consider those 3-D pictures that you often find in newspapers. On the surface they don't look like much, but keep looking and all at once an image will appear. That's the real picture—what's inside. Look carefully at the unpleasant or difficult child in your classroom to see the real picture—what's inside.

Children want a productive environment. They don't want to waste their time, and they don't want to be someplace where the teacher is always frustrated. Kids want limits on their behavior and that of others. They need an environment that is controlled, but not controlling. They need positive limits but they don't want to be held to impossible standards. Here are questions to ask yourself about the environment in your class:

- Am I consistent?
- Do I have a clear routine?
- Do I let my class know what I expect of them?
- Are any of the children in my class afraid of me?
- Do I ever try to show my power?
- Can my kids ask an honest question and get an honest answer?
- Do I encourage or inhibit certain behaviors?
- Do I promote cooperation and healthy competition?
- How do I handle noise?
- How do I handle mistakes? Interruptions?
- Do I favor one child over another?
- Do I treat each child fairly based on their needs and abilities?

Review your answers from time to time to help keep on track.

Kids want you to be relevant. This is especially important in religion class. The message of faith needs to be presented so that it means something to *them*—to their lives, not yours; to their world, not yours.

We need to get into their world and make use of the things that they can relate to. Learn their language; try to understand it, and be able to interpret it. Remember what it is like to be their age, and that the world in which they live is different from our own childhood world. I grew up with Elvis Presley, black-and-white TV, and dial phones. My children grew up with the new-wave band the Cars, space travel, and the cassette Walkman. My grandchildren are growing up with hip-hop, a global economy, iPods, and the Internet. These are not just generation gaps. It is a whole new world.

Each generation has a culture unto itself. We must treat their culture with respect for it is the world to which they belong. Tread carefully. Don't dismiss it. This is the culture in which God is revealing himself to *this* generation. Baby boomers are different from those who lived through the Depression; Generation Xers are different from the children born today. Each has its wisdom, and we need to respect that. God doesn't speak only in the language of thirty-or forty-or fifty-year-olds. He speaks in the language of the young. Help the kids to listen for it.

Use examples from their customs and from their lives. The older the student, the more important this becomes. It is too easy for us to dismiss their culture as meaningless or secondary to our own. Rather, show them where God lives in their world today. Teach them what they need to know to become better Catholic Christians now—and give them the principles they will need to live as a Christian tomorrow.

Sometimes at the end of the religion class, you can almost sense the kids saying, "So what?" Show them how to apply religion to their everyday life. What difference do *your* words make in *my* life? Use life to teach. What is going on in the world in which these children live? What issues are they facing? How does the Gospel speak to those issues? What are Christians called upon to do in the world of the twenty-first century?

Kids would like you to be clairvoyant. Hear what they *aren't* saying. In the television series *M*A*S*H,* Radar got his nickname because he could always intuit what a person wanted or needed before they told him what it was. We need to have that same radar as we teach.

"Notice how I look today. Look at me carefully. What do you see? Pick up my messages. Do I look troubled? Did my parents just have a fight? Was I picked on by the other kids at school today? Am I hungry? Tired? Was it somebody's birthday and I wasn't invited to the party? Do I feel like I'm not as good as everyone else?" What are the children telling you without words? And how can you help?

Do they need affirmation? Reassurance? Encouragement? Be aware of the children in front of you and be there for them when you can help.

Sometimes our children live in situations that are hard for us to imagine. Some are hungry; some are left alone; some are not cared for; some are unloved. Some are treated harshly; some are neglected; some are ridiculed. Some carry burdens that are hard for them to bear. Most of us cannot change their world. But we can do one thing.

When that child enters your room, you are in charge. You set the tone. You can create a place of respect and peace, acceptance and affirmation, and a place where, perhaps, the child can feel the love and strength of God reaching out to him.

Kids wish that you understood the great power that you have. You are the teacher. Your words and attitude can build them up or break them down, encourage them or discourage them, hurt them or heal them, inspire them or squelch them, set them free or bind them up, help them grow or put them down. And, because you have that power, they want you to remember to be gentle with them. Remember that they are fragile and vulnerable, trusting and sometimes afraid, and always in the process of becoming. It is our job to understand them, love them, and pray for them.

And Finally…

The list of things that are important for a catechist to know sometimes seems endless. There are developmental stages, classroom-management issues, theological questions, and on and on. There are also thousands upon thousands of ideas and suggestions to use with children. It's hard to know where to begin. So, here is a list of randomly chosen ideas, suggestions, techniques, activities, and reminders, framed within the ABCs. Use it as a starting point to spark your own creativity.

AN ALPHABET FOR NEW CATECHISTS

A is for audience. Consider them carefully. Who are they? What are they like? What are their interests and their needs? How can we present the message in a way that they can understand it? We have something important to say to them, but unless we pay attention to the audience who is to receive the message, they will never get it. If I speak Spanish in Germany, there is little chance that they will understand what I'm saying.

Jesus always considered his audience when he was speaking to the people of his time. With fisherman he spoke of fish, and told them that they would be fishers of men. With farmers, he spoke of seeds and compared them with the word of God. With shepherds he spoke of sheep and told them that he was the good shepherd. He used things that were familiar to him as examples so his message was easy for them to understand.

B is for begin. Begin your class productively. From the moment the children walk into the room, use the time well. Have something on their desks or on the board that they can begin working on even before class begins. This can be a simple activity and might be one that could be used during the first part of the lesson. Or it might be a quick review of the previous week's work. Or perhaps they could write a prayer, or complete a sentence. For example, "If I could have one wish, it would be...," or, "I would like to visit..." Use a different idea each week and get the class off to a good start.

C is for Christ. He is at the center of what we do. Don't ever lose sight of that fact while you are in the midst of educational principles and catechetical documents. No book, no technique, no process should ever be seen as more important than simply helping the children to learn to love the Lord.

D is for discipline. You can't teach without it. Set clear standards of acceptable behavior in your class. Be realistic in your expectations, be sure your class understands them, and be sure to adhere to them faithfully and consistently.

Keep the children actively involved in the lesson with meaningful projects geared to their level of understanding and ability. Following these principles you should have few if any discipline problems in your class.

E is for envelopes. Kids like to get mail, so send them some thing: a certificate for learning the Ten Commandments or a prayer; a card or a set of stickers; best of all, a note telling them something that you enjoy about them. Praise goes a long way, and when it is written down, it can be kept and read over and over.

F is for field trips. Do one each year. Tour the local synagogue with a class that is studying the Old Testament. Take a class to the cathedral, perhaps even to an ordination. Take students to a soup kitchen or a food bank, or the rectory or a local monastery, or just outside where your prayer group has set up the Stations of the Cross.

Be creative and find someplace interesting to visit as a change of pace from the classroom. You may find the children remember it more than almost anything else you did all year. Plus, it's a great way to get parents involved as chaperones and drivers.

G is for goal. Having a goal gives you direction and focus and gives it to your students as well. Plan your year with your calendar in hand. Know when Advent and Lent start; when classes are not in session; when you'll take your field trip; when you want to do your service project; when you want to invite in a guest speaker, and so on. It's amazing how much you can accomplish when you have a goal and a plan to accomplish it.

H is for help. Use any and all things that will help you to become a better teacher. Start a teacher team. Divide the workload. Partner with a more experienced teacher. Don't be afraid to ask questions. Enlist help from others. Is there someone who does desktop publishing who can create great activity sheets or certificates for you? A drama person who can help plan and stage a play? An arts and crafts person who can design and create projects? Get them involved in your planning or in your class for something special.

I is for individual. Get to know each child in your class as an individual. Learn about him or her. What does he like to do? What are her special talents? See each child as unique and special. Greet each child as he or she arrives at class. Call each child by name. At the end of class each week pray for each individual child by name.

Give each child a chance to shine. Help each child to feel that they are an important part of your class. When a child is absent, let him or her know that you missed them. Look for the good and affirm each child whenever you can.

J is for job. You've taken on an important one. Treat it as such. Be on time, be prepared to teach, have your materials ready, and be there each and every week, even when you'd rather be doing something else. Get the training you need to do the best job possible. Spend the time needed to get the job done right. Commit yourself to it.

As the saying goes, "Work for the Lord. The pay isn't much, but the rewards are heavenly."

K is for the kids' wish list.
- I wish you would make the class more interesting so that the hour would go faster.
- I wish you would call on me first, just once.
- I wish you wouldn't ask me to read.
- I wish you would just let me sharpen my pencil without acting like it is a big deal.
- I wish you had a sense of humor.
- I wish you would explain things twice—just to be sure I understand.
- I wish you would spend some time asking me about *me.*
- I wish you would say something nice about me in front of the other kids.
- I wish you would understand that sometimes I just can't pay attention.

L is for laughter. Keep your sense of humor. It will save many a day. Have fun with your class. Don't take everything so seriously. A teacher I know was having a terrible day with her senior class. She was tired and the class just didn't settle down. The students were talking, paying no attention, and driving her crazy. Finally, knowing that it was absolutely the wrong way to handle the situation, she lost her temper. She yelled at them. In the middle of her tirade, she paused to take a breath. A girl in the front row, in what was supposed to be a show of support shouted out, "You tell 'em Mrs. M!" After a second of silence, ripples of laughter began to fill the room. Mrs. M found herself laughing right along with her class at the absurdity of the situation. The laughter defused the tension and her anger. The students calmed down, the air was cleared, and the rest of the class continued as it should.

Laughter is the gift that helps us to take things into perspective, to see what is trivial and what is really important. Laughter, especially when we can laugh at ourselves, goes a long way in helping us keep our perspective. As Mrs. M learned, it is a great equalizer.

M is for make and take. Sometimes the religious symbol or banner that we make in religion class is the only religious item visible in the home. Start a tradition in your class by making one item a year that can be taken home and displayed.

The following craft is quick and easy. The directions show how to make a cross, but the bread can be shaped into any symbol.

For each child you will need—
    A slice of white bread
    One tablespoon of white glue
    One paper cup
    One craft stick
    Sheet of waxed paper to cover work surface

Directions
1. Tear crust off bread. Break bread into small pieces and put them into cup.
2. Add glue to cup and mix with wooden stick.
3. Knead with hands until soft dough forms.

4. Roll dough into 2 four-inch strips and 2 six-inch strips.
5. Twist the 2 six-inch strips together. Then twist the 2 four-inch strips together. Put one on top of the other to make a cross shape. Press *lightly*.
6. Let dry. Hang by thread or floss.

N is for never. Never be afraid to ask a question or to tell the class that you don't know the answer. Never give up, even in February when it seems like the year will never end. Never become a catechist if you don't really, really like kids. It just won't work. Never teach from your own agenda. And most important, never doubt that the Lord is with you always, no matter where, no matter when.

O is for other. Watch other teachers. See how it is done. We learn a lot by watching others. Yet often we have teachers in our religion classes who have never actually seen a class of their grade level being taught. If you're one of them, see if you can arrange to sit in on a class. Ask if you can observe in a Catholic school class, or sit in on a lesson in a public school. You will learn a lot about both teaching and learning by watching.

P is for possibilities. When you look at a child, look at the possibilities. That's what Jesus did. When he called Zacchaeus down from the tree, he saw more than the tax collector. He saw a person with possibilities, one who could change and learn from what he had done wrong. And so, having met and talked with Jesus, Zacchaeus was transformed into a new person. Jesus saw the good in people and drew it out.

Don't only see what the children are now. See what they *can* be, and help them to see it too. A man with an unusual talent visited an agent one day. When the agent asked what he could do, the man replied, "I can do bird imitations." The agent said, "Get out of here! Bird imitators are a dime a dozen." With that the man flew out of the window. Look underneath the obvious and you may just get a surprise.

Q is for quiet. Times of silence are important both in your classroom and in your life. We live in a noisy world. This is especially true for children. There is great wisdom in a phrase from the psalms "Be still and know that I am God." Help your students experience silence in prayer. Help them to learn to listen to God speaking to them in the quiet of their own heart. Before you pray with them each week, pause for a moment until they are still and calm and ready to center themselves on God.

R is for reflection. When we look into a mirror, we see ourselves reflected back to us. When we look at others, they also reflect back to us, the person whom they see us to be. We learn who we are from other people's reactions to us. It is like we are holding up a little mirror in which they can see themselves. If we mirror back frustration, a child begins to see himself as incompetent or in the way. If we mirror back affirmation, the child begins to see himself as competent and capable.

Your facial expressions and body language say a lot to a child. Be sure that you are sending the right messages.

S is for story. Everyone loves stories. They are a marvelous teaching tool. They have a universal appeal and convey a message or insight like few other things do.

Make it a point to use stories whenever possible. And don't be afraid to use them in the upper grades as well. Get to know the children's librarian at your local library. He or she can be a wonderful resource for classic and new books. Browse through the children's section of Christian bookstores for a wealth of stories you can use in your class.

T is for training. Gold-medal athletes continue to train even after they have won. Although they are acknowledged as the best, they continue to practice and to learn as much as they can about their sport. They look for new ways to do better. So should we. We are always in training, both in teaching and in being a Christian.

Take advantage of the opportunities to attend courses and conferences that will help you to be a better catechist. Attend catechist meetings. Read catechetical magazines. Continue to grow as a catechist.

U is for understanding. Understand the world in which your children live. Understand who and what they are. Understand where they are in their development: academically, physically, and emotionally. Treat them with kindness.

All children should leave your class feeling better about themselves, feeling as though they have been a part of something good, feeling that *they* are good, even when others may tell them differently.

V is for vision. We share with the children a vision of a world that is better than we have now. We are a people of hope. We know that Jesus has gone to prepare a place for us. We know that, because Jesus died for us, we will live with him for all eternity.

Keep alive the vision of heaven. We don't always tell kids enough about it. We were created not just for this world, but for what comes next.

W is for wealth of resources. No matter what you are looking for today, you can find it online in a matter of seconds. As a catechist looking for ideas and information it is an amazing resource. Looking for the *Catechism of the Catholic Church*? Check out the American Bishops' Web site at www.usccb.com. It's all there, along with the *New American Bible,* news releases, statements and addresses, movie reviews, and lots more.

All of the major religious publishers have their own Web sites. Many of these have activity sheets, stories, current events, Gospel reflections, and more. Take advantage of all that these Web sites have to offer. There's always something new and something worthwhile.

X is for eXtemporaneous. There is no substitute for planning your lessons, but don't be a slave to your plan. Sometimes you will find the students have a question or want to discuss another topic. If it is appropriate, go with it. Perhaps there is something in the newspaper or on the news about capital punishment or another moral issue. Take advantage of the opportunity to use this current event. Listen to the children's concerns and questions.

Help your students see how and where the message of Jesus applies to the situation.

From time to time you will also find that the students' interest is sparked by a particular area of study. If so, continue with it. If they're interested in what you're teaching, they're learning.

Y is for Yes. The attitude of *yes* is a scary approach to life. Yet its openness allows the impossible to become possible. If your arms are closed with fear and nay-saying, they can't be open to receive the unexpected. So open your arms and begin to trust. Some initial desire to be a catechist brought you to this point. Now, say to yourself and believe: *Yes,* you can teach! *Yes,* your class will learn! *Yes,* both you and your class can have an inspiring, enjoyable, even *fun* experience. Expect that *your* yes will be answered with a yes.

Z is for Zeal. The apostles were full of zeal, full of enthusiasm, on that Pentecost morning once they felt the Spirit of the Lord come upon them. The Book of Acts and Paul's own letters reveal his zeal to bring the message of Jesus to the world. Even shipwrecks and prison couldn't diminish his eagerness to spread the Good News.

It is this same spirit of zeal that brings you back to class week after week, even when you are tired and discouraged. You see a job to be done and you do it. The world is a better place because Martin Luther King didn't say, "I don't do marches." And because Mother Teresa didn't say, "I don't do the dying." And because Jesus didn't say, "I don't do crosses." And because *you* didn't say, "I don't do sixth grade." Someone's world will be a better place because you do.

"BUT I'M NOT REALLY ALL THAT RELIGIOUS…"

None of us is comfortable with the knowledge that we are models of faith and of Jesus to the children. But knowing it makes us able to do something about it. Kids spot a fake. They demand that we practice what we preach. If we talk about kindness, then we'd better be kind. If we talk about peace, then we'd better control our anger. If we introduce them to Jesus, then we'd better know him well ourselves. If we profess to be Catholic, then we need to be Catholic in more than just name. We can't ask more of our students than we do of ourselves.

As we sit and think about these things, many of us experience a sense of discomfort. Some of us have let our relationship with God stagnate or slip. What then?

When I was a child I had a friend named Carolyn. She was the daughter of one of my parents' closest friends. We spent a lot of time together: Sundays, holidays, birthdays. We were very close. Carolyn was an extremely important part of my life. We shared all of our joys, our sorrows, and a lot of just ordinary days.

As we grew older and went away to college, got married, and had our own children—Carolyn and I drifted apart. We still saw each other at weddings and funerals and once in a while on Christmas or Thanksgiving. But we really weren't as close as we were. After our parents died, our relationship became one of Christmas cards with short notes: "It would be great to get together again…

someday." Carolyn had been such an important part of my life, and now I seldom even thought about her. We hadn't had a fight. It was just that she was no longer a part of my everyday life. We had lost what we had, a deep and, what should have been, a lasting friendship.

One day I decided to do something about it. I got on the phone and called her up. When she answered the phone, she knew immediately who it was. Her first words were, "It is so wonderful to hear your voice. I've missed you so much." It took just a few seconds for us to reconnect and realize what we had been missing.

Our relationship with God might be a lot like my relationship with Carolyn. God was an important part of our childhood. We went to church on Sundays, celebrated the sacraments, knew the presence of God in our joys and sorrows and all the ordinary times of life. But as the years went by, we lost that sense of God walking with us, being with us. Maybe we stopped praying, or stopped attending Mass other than on Christmas and Easter. We still believed in God. We still spoke of him in times of illness or death. But we had drifted apart. We knew that God was still there, but he was no longer a part of our everyday life. We had lost what we had, a deep and lasting friendship.

Maybe it is time to get back in touch with God. Call him. He will recognize your voice, and you will be met with "It's so wonderful to hear from you! I've missed you so much." And it is like the years in between disappear. Worth thinking about?

ONE FINAL STORY

Shortly after Jesus went back to heaven, a group of angels asked him how things had gone on earth. Jesus replied that it had gone pretty well. The angels asked Jesus who would spread his message now that he was back in heaven. Jesus pointed down to earth, to Peter and Thomas and the other apostles. The angels were aghast. "You mean you are entrusting the future to them? What happens if they don't do it?" To which Jesus replied, "I have no other plans."

Peter...Paul...St. Francis...Thomas Aquinas...Augustine ...Ignatius of Loyola...Elizabeth Seton...John XXIII... Sister Mary Elizabeth...Mrs. M...and now you.

OTHER BOOKS IN THIS SERIES

Connecting with Parents
Mary Twomey Spollen

Praying with Young People
Maureen Gallagher